Pain I Must Endure

Danise Donerson

Copyright © 2023 Danise Donerson
All rights reserved
First Edition

PAGE PUBLISHING
Conneaut Lake, PA

First originally published by Page Publishing 2023

ISBN 978-1-6624-8790-3 (pbk)
ISBN 979-8-88793-185-2 (hc)
ISBN 978-1-6624-8789-7 (digital)

Printed in the United States of America

In loving memory of my mama, Dorothy A. Toran, and dad, Walter C. Griffin.

Contents

Preface vii
Acknowledgments ix
Chapter 1:   Our First Introduction 1
Chapter 2:   My Life of Pain Began 6
Chapter 3:   The Failed Surgery 10
Chapter 4:   The Nightmare Began 14
Chapter 5:   My Silent Cry 19
Chapter 6:   The First Year of Pain 23
Chapter 7:   My Acceptance 27
Chapter 8:   The Unforeseen Pain 30
Chapter 9:   My Feeling of Abandonment 35
Chapter 10: My Faith 37
Chapter 11: A Lifetime of Pain 40
Chapter 12: Oh, My Israelite Sistas 43
Chapter 13: My Intense Therapy 50
Chapter 14: Pain You Are Evicted! 53

Preface

This book was written to inspire and encourage anyone that is suffering from any kind of pain to never give up hope. I realize that pain comes in many forms; mine was physical and psychological; this is my journey and struggle with the horrific pain from many failed back surgeries. How I coped and sought help spiritually from God's Word. Also, how I refused to give up hope for relief. By keeping my faith in check.

Acknowledgments

I would like to thank my Israel of God Church Family worldwide. I specifically want to thank the following people that have been there for me during a very challenging time in my life: David Donerson, my husband. To Sister Tiara Redd, Brother Victor Johnson, and my IOG Family in Jackson, Mississippi. Brother James Anderson at the IOG in Hayward, California, The late Derek Johnson of Knoxville, Tennessee, Brother Kevin Israel at the IOG in St. Louis, Missouri, Sister Margaret Cobb in Jackson, Mississippi, Sister Drew Israel in Chicago, Illinois, at the IOG in Riverdale, Illinois, Sister Cheryl Thomas at the IOG in Dallas, Texas, Sister Key Israel in Virginia. Just to name a few people. There were more, and I thank you all.

I would like to thank the IOG in Riverdale, Illinois, for their support during my illness.

I thank three of my awesome friends, Mildred Butler, Maggie White, and Staniece Studaway. I love you all with all my heart. Thanks for the monetary gifts and prayers from my church family.

I want to thank my wonderful surgeon Dr. Benjamin Kerr and his staff for trying to fix what other doctors couldn't, in my opinion.

I would like to thank the physical and occupational therapists, nurses, and techs who helped me through my intense therapy at the Methodist Rehabilitation Hospital. This book is for every reader that is going through pain twenty-four-seven nonstop! May God bring you all through, like me. Stay prayerful, and keep the faith in Christ Jesus.

The Butterflies throughout this book is in memory of my mother. She was with me for every doctor's appointment, hospital stay and surgery. Even though she was ill herself. Now she is free of her pain and the cares of this world. Like a beautiful butterfly flying free in the wind.

CHAPTER 1
Our First Introduction

It was early in the morning on November 2, 2012; I was waiting to vote. It was President Obama's second election. It was a cloudy, dreary morning. I was standing in line with my daughter Kenya. While standing in line, I had the most excruciating pain that went down my leg. I called the doctor's office to get some pain medicine called into the pharmacy. The pain traveled down my leg slowly. By the end of the day, it was worse than anything that I had ever experienced in my life. I had to take Kenya back to school; she came home to vote. I needed her to drive, but the 5:00 p.m. traffic was heavy. I decided to drive. This was the longest two-hour trip to her college. I was hurting so bad that I had crocodile tears running down my face. I didn't want her to know that I was hurting.

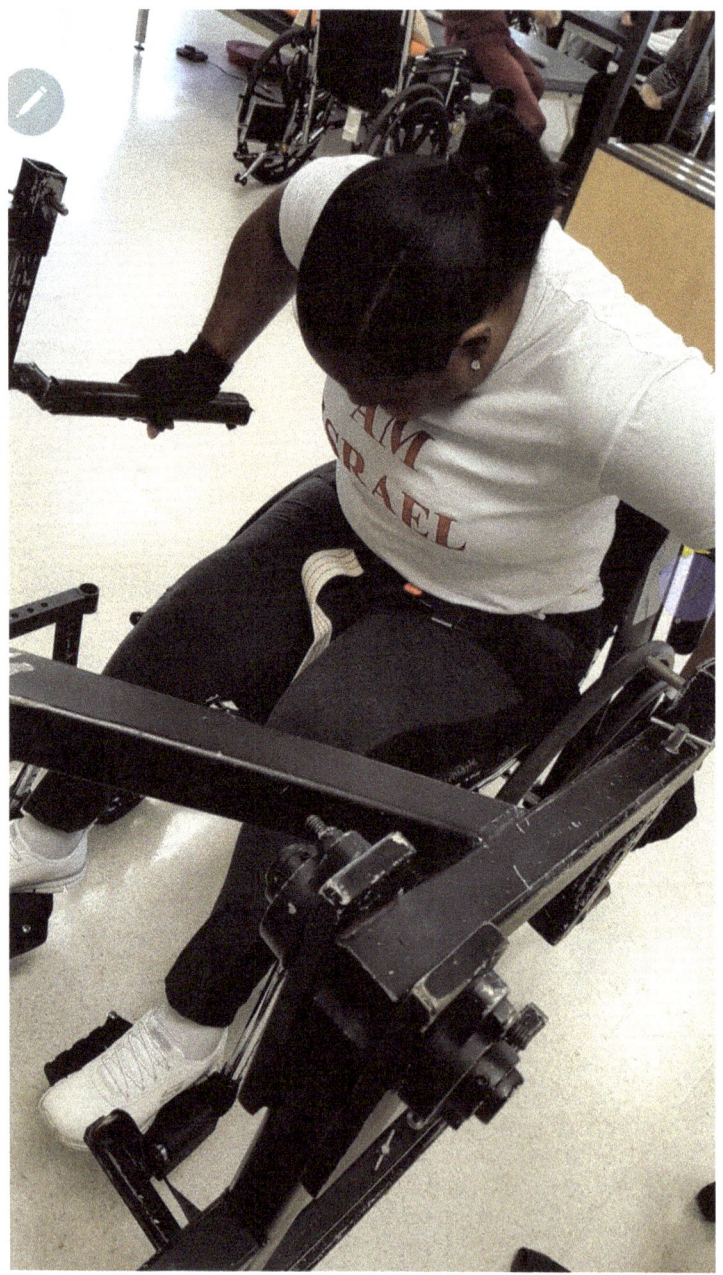

Philippians 4:13 KJV I can do all things through Christ which strengtheneth me.

Shoot, I was so scared that I didn't want her to worry about me. Once I dropped her off, my grandson Tazz helped her with her bags. I immediately got back onto the highway headed back to my town. I couldn't feel my right leg; however, I did feel this shooting pain down my right leg. It was so weird but extremely painful. I had my two grandsons in the back seat; I was so scared I called my oldest daughter, Kendra. I told her That I couldn't feel my right leg. She asked where I was, and I honestly didn't know. It was very dark; eighteen-wheelers were passing my car. I couldn't feel my foot; I felt only a dull pressure.

So I tried to keep the speed of the traffic on the highway. Pain had taken over me. I kept driving until I came to a deep curve and sudden bright lights. I realized what town I was in. I pulled over into the parking lot of a gas station. I turned the car off, I looked over into traffic, and there was an ambulance at the red light. I was so delirious with pain and weak that I couldn't move. I called Kendra to tell her the name of the town that the boys and I were in. She and my son-in-law came to pick me and the boys up.

Once they made it to us, he picked me up and put me on the passenger side of my Honda two-door sports car. Oh my, it was so low, and the pain had totally taken over me. I told Kendra to take me to UMMC Hospital for pain management. Once I was there, I was hurting so bad my blood pressure was so high; they took me straight back to a room in the ER. I was hurting so bad I couldn't lie down on my right side. So I held on for dear life to the rail of the bed while the nurses and doctors talked to me.

My face was about three inches from the wall, literally. I was scheduled to have a spinal injection that Thursday. So I told the doctors to give me pain management. The pain was so great that the pain medicine that they gave me didn't work. While in the ER, lying on a stretcher, they announced that President Obama won his second election. What a place to be; I was discharged home. Pain was trying to take over my body and, eventually, my life.

I went Tuesday and Wednesday with a ruptured disc. Every time I tried to get up to walk, it was as if my right leg was not there. Fear really set in; I didn't know what to do. Thursday morning came, my mama took me to my appointment to get the Spinal injection. While sitting in the waiting room, there were two other patients. We all had the same appointment time. I don't know what look I had on my face; one of the patients was a preacher. He came and kneeled down beside me and asked me if he could pray for me. I said sure; once he finished, the nurse had called my name.

The other patients both said at the same time, "She can't walk that far, she needs a wheelchair."

I politely thanked them both once I was put in the wheelchair. Oh my, I hurt so bad it got worse by the second. The nurse put me in a room. Everybody that passed the door looked at me and said, "I'm so sorry that you are in so much pain."

The doctor passed my door and said, "Uh…whatever I was going to do today is not going to help you." He instructed my mama to take me to the St. Dominic Hospital for an emergency MRI. The nurses and my mama asked if he wanted them to call the ambulance. He said, "No, help her into the car and take her."

PAIN I MUST ENDURE

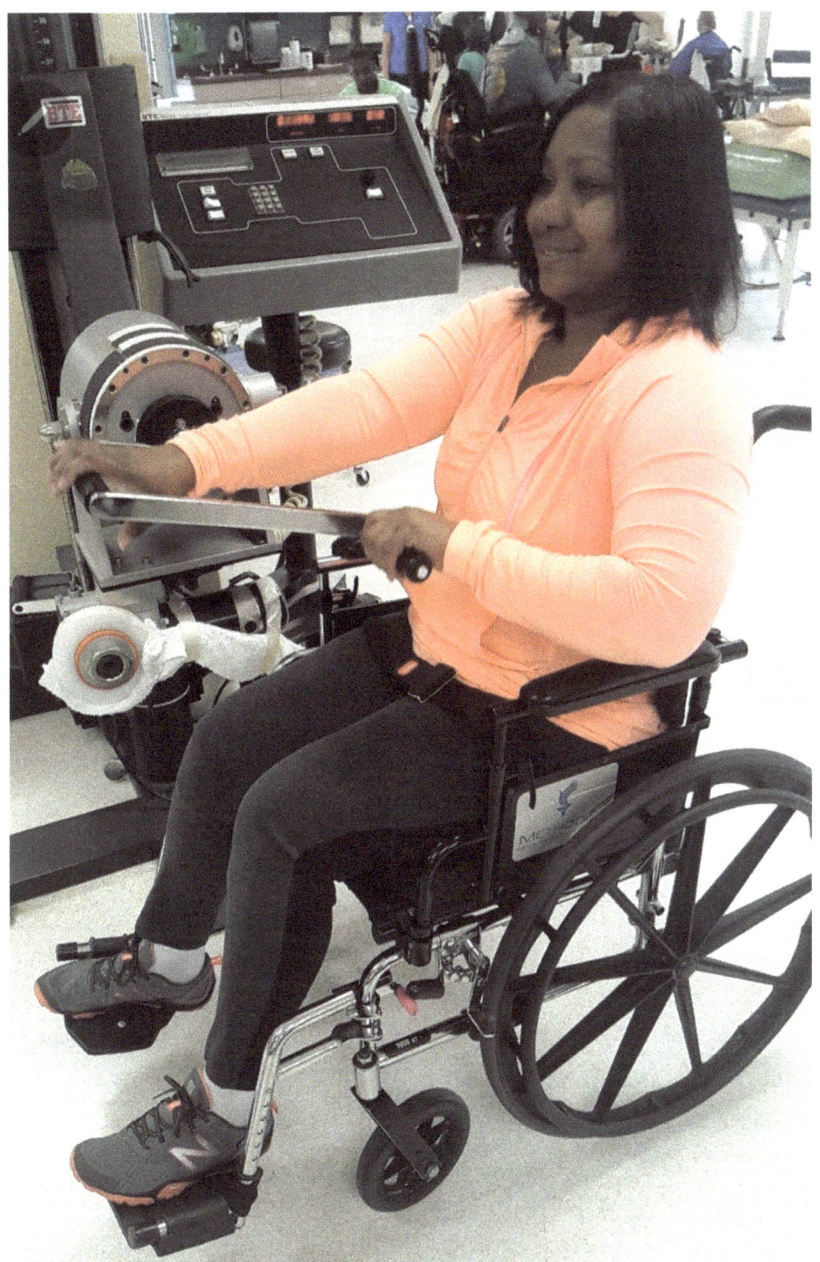

Roman 12:12 KJV Rejoicing in hope; patient in tribulation; continuing instant in prayer;

Chapter 2
My Life of Pain Began

On November 8, 2012, I entered pain's door. I was hurting so bad. The admissions clerk felt so bad for me. She was trying to get me admitted as fast as possible. However, she had to give me the bad news that there weren't any beds available in the whole hospital. While I was waiting, she sent me to get my lab work and x-rays done.

The nurse didn't know the severity of my pain. She asked me to try and stand; *oh my God*! I asked her if I could hug the machine; I couldn't stand at all. Another nurse was passing the door; she looked into my room and said, "Uh…you need a stretcher." She got the stretcher, and they allowed me to try and rest until a room was available.

It took eight hours before I was put into a room. I was hurting so bad, delirious in pain. I found a spot on the stretcher that I was able to fall asleep for a brief moment. I must have moved because the pain had awakened me out of my little nap. I kept asking my mama to check to see if there was a room available. Sadly, there wasn't a bed; she asked about three times.

Finally, there was a room available; I thanked God. The admitting nurse was trying to get my medical history. I remembered that I had to have an emergency MRI; I immediately reminded the nurse that I was claustrophobic and that she had to knock me out with some type of pain medication. If I had awakened out of my sleep in that machine, I would become an instant psych patient. I just couldn't lie on my right side, period. I went to have my MRI, and Oh my... I awoke for a few seconds after my hand hit the side of the machine.

When I did wake up, I was back in my room. The nurse told me that my disc had ruptured into chunks! I was told by the nurse that I had to have emergency surgery. At that moment, I didn't care; I wanted the severe sciatic nerve pain to stop now! Any means necessary, period!

Luke 1:37 KJV For with God nothing shall be impossible. Even though the pain was great the nurses had to inject me with pain medication before each therapy session that lasted three hours each day. I knew that I had to do this for myself. I had to totally trust God no matter what!

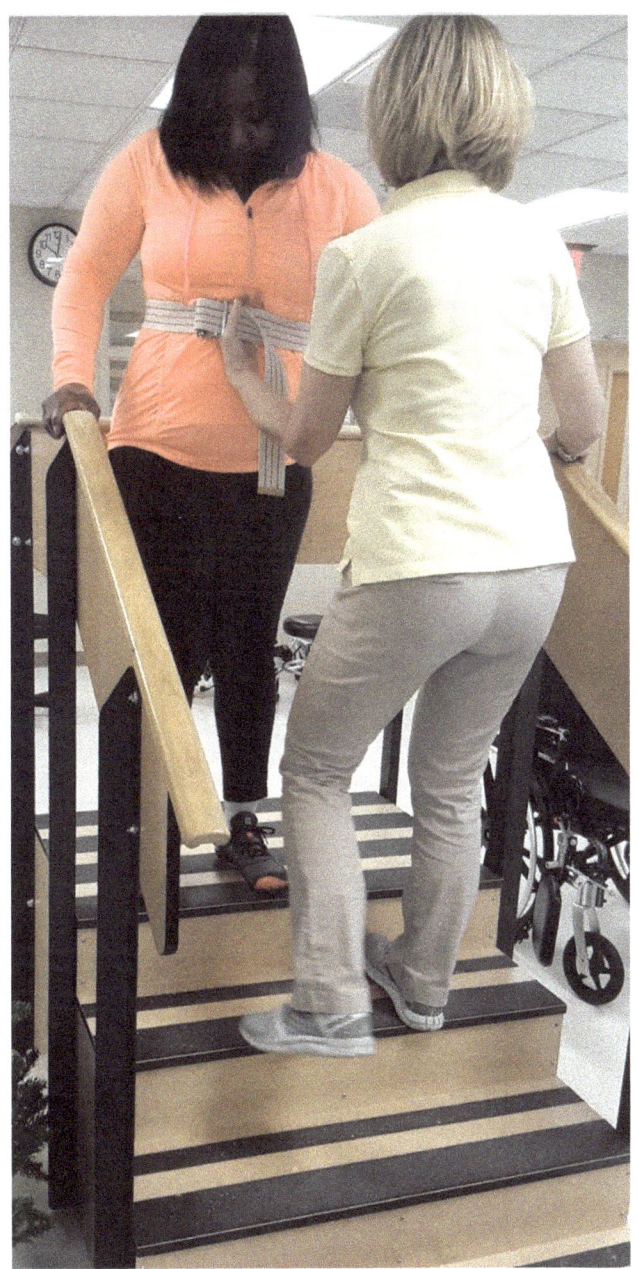

This was my hardest challenge. It took me over two years to walk up and down stairs without severe pain in my back.

Chapter 3

The Failed Surgery

Once the test came back that I had to have emergency surgery, I was put on NPO, nothing by mouth. I was drugged up with plenty of pain medication. I was awakened around 5:00 a.m. to take a shower in a special solution. However, something was wrong, time went by, and no one came to take me to surgery.

I remember waking up and looking over at my mama. The doctor was talking to her, but no one said anything to me. Time went by; I continued to wake up periodically, still drugged up. Finally, I felt like it was late. So I asked my mama were they going to reschedule the surgery? Also, I stated, "Mama, they must be going to reschedule the surgery because they are going to be tired by the time they get to me."

Shortly after I made that statement to my mama, a guy came in and said that he was going to wheel me down to surgery. Once I was taken down to the surgery floor. I awakened again, but I was surrounded by equipment like beds and monitors, etc. I looked around, and I felt scared. No one was watching me. Suddenly, I had to go to the restroom. I began to panic; I raised up a little, I saw the back of a nurse sitting a few feet away from me.

I kept saying, "Ma'am…," in this very distressful low voice.

She finally heard me calling her. She came over to me and said, "Yes, may I help you?"

I said, "Yes, can you please help me to the restroom."

She helped me back into my bed. She left and went back to her area. I began to hurt so bad; I guess that the pain medicine had worn off. I was holding on to the rail of the bed for dear life, it seemed. Suddenly, a man appeared beside my bed.

He said, "You look like you are in a lot of pain. Would you like me to give you something for the pain or something to make you not care?"

I said, "Something to make me not care!"

He turned out to be the anesthesiologist. I was taken to the operating room. I remember looking at one of the nurses or tech's face, and he looked very tired. The last thing that I remember was people turning me over onto my stomach on the weird table. When I awakened, I was so excited!

I said, "Mama, call my children that pain was gone."

She said, "We can't call anybody, it's too early in the morning!" While shoving Jell-O into my mouth. It had been about nineteen hours since I had eaten or had anything to drink. My excitement was short-lived! Sadly, the pain came back with a vengeance.

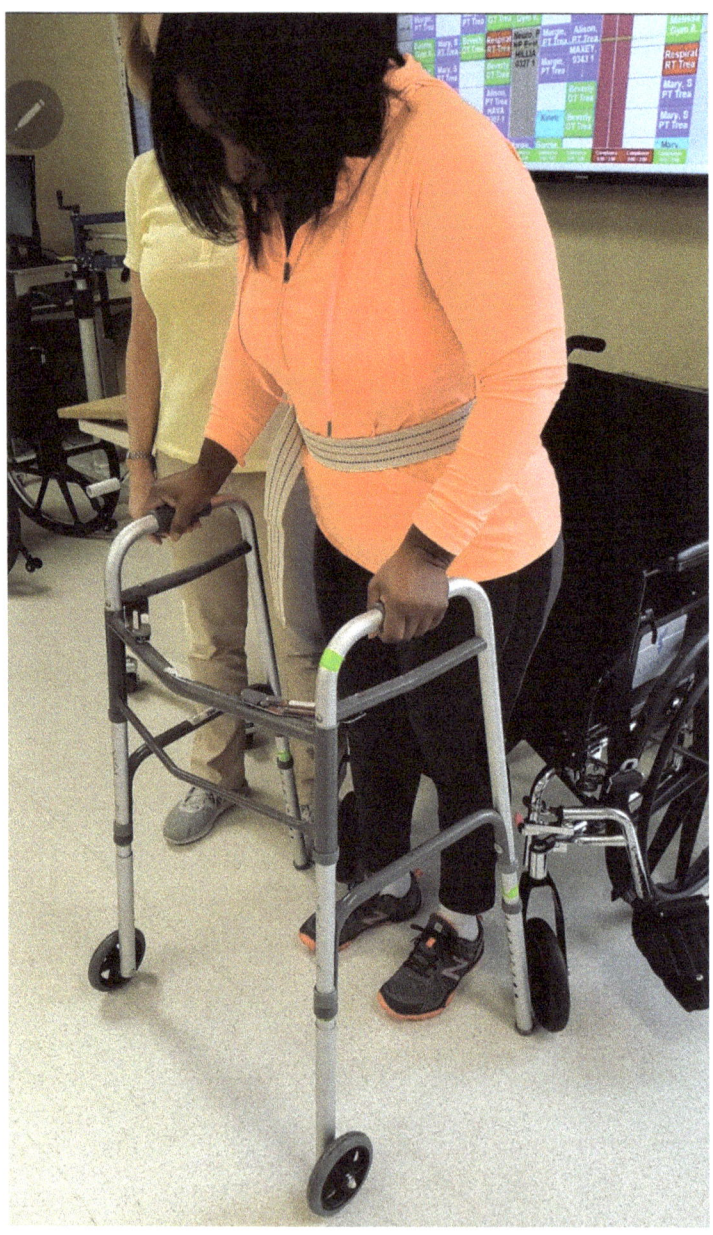

I was learning to use my upper body strength to use the walker to take each step. My legs were extremely weak from my back surgeries and screws.

PAIN I MUST ENDURE

I was learning how to sit down and get up using my thighs.

CHAPTER 4

The Nightmare Began

I was admitted into the hospital on November 8 and discharged on November 12. Every shift after the surgery, I kept complaining of right leg pain. My pain level was a ten, and I kept asking for pain medication. They discharged me home with severe right leg pain. Two weeks later, I had a follow-up with the surgeon. I told him that I couldn't feel my four right toes. He immediately told my mama to take me to have another emergency MRI.

She took me to an imaging facility; I had been there before. I had told my mama to drop me off and go pick up my grandsons from school. I went inside to check in, and the lady was so rude and told me that they couldn't see me because I had a balance. However, I wasn't aware of the balance, nor did I have the money to pay it because I wasn't working. I informed her that doctor sent me there for an emergency MRI. She said that I was not going to be seen unless the balance was paid. I walked outside crying and in pain.

I had forgotten that my mama had left. I called her cell phone. Thankfully, she was still at the light because of the traffic. She immediately came back. I called the doctor's office, and he instructed me to go to the St. Dominic Hospital for my MRI. I had about eight MRIs in a year. I started researching for myself. I found a device that could be put in between my disc that had ruptured. It was manufactured in Germany. My next doctor appointment, I couldn't wait to share the news with him. Unfortunately, the FDA hadn't approved it for the states.

Once the doctors saw that I had been researching my condition and other opinions. He asked me to sit at his computer with him. He stated that he knew that you would be back. I really didn't understand what that meant. He showed me a model of a neurostimulator. This device would be placed on my spine and a battery at the base of my back. This implant would be for pain management. I had to wait about two weeks before the second doctor/specialist was going to implant the device and review my records.

During this process, I was hurting so bad; I was delirious in pain. I had to pass a psychiatric test before the insurance company would pay $20,000 for the temporary implant. While waiting for the implant, I became extremely depressed. I remembered getting my calendar, and I counted the number of days that I had been hurting. It totaled 270-plus days.

My oldest daughter took me to my appointment with the specialist. I had to fill out paperwork before being seen. I admitted that I was depressed. The nurse practitioner saw something in my chart that alerted her to share it with the doctor. Afterward, the nurse practitioner stated that the doctor was referring me back to the original surgeon. All of this after getting approved by the insurance company. A red flag was raised in my mind. However, I was so drugged up and in severe pain. I had to wait another two weeks for another specialist to review my medical records. Now, I was still hurting nonstop, twenty-four-seven in severe pain. I kept calling the first surgeon's office to let them know that I was in excruciating pain. They kept telling me to wait until the third doctor called me for an appointment.

I was tired of crying, screaming, and hurting. It was as if the pain was taking over my mind. I could relate to people that had committed suicide. I started texting people that I thought loved me. I texted that I couldn't take it anymore. Immediately, people started texting me back, "Are you okay?"

My oldest daughter called me and said, "Ma, what's wrong?"

I told her that I wanted her to take me to the hospital where I had my back surgery. Also, I was not leaving until someone helped me. She repeated what I had told her.

Once I felt that we were on the same page, I said, "Okay, I will see you in the morning."

I got out of bed. I went into the kitchen, and I reached above the stove into the cabinet. I got a bottle of Jack Daniel's liquor, and I poured about four ounces into a glass. Now how I was able to reach up into the cabinet is a mystery to me until this day. I had the most peaceful sleep. The Lord allowed me to wake up the next morning. It was nobody but him because I was on so much narcotic medication to kill a horse.

The next morning, my daughter picked me up from home and took me to the hospital that did my surgery. While in the triage room, I told the nurse that I needed her to hear me. I love my family, and I didn't have suicidal ideations. However, I did drink some strong liquor, knowing that I had narcotic medication in my system.

I was in chronic pain, and I came back here for help. She immediately stated that this changes things. She took me back to a trauma room. I pleaded with the ER doctor and nurses. I informed them that I was in chronic pain, and I had been hurting for over *270-plus* days nonstop, twenty-four-seven with no relief. They immediately took my clothes, gave me one pain pill, and gave me some scrubs to put on. They wouldn't let me see or speak to my daughter. The nightmare really began to set in. I was admitted into a mental behavior hospital.

I was strengthening my upper body to help support my lower body that was extremely weak.

CHAPTER 5

My Silent Cry

Once I was admitted into the mental behavior hospital. I began to cry silently. I was so tired of hurting and crying; the pain was so controlling that it was a part of my daily life. The pain had me crippled; I couldn't stand to walk. I was so delirious in pain. I couldn't think; I began to talk to it as if was a person. Ironically, the patients were pushing me back and forth to my room. It was time to take my night medicine.

The nurse looked at me and said, you look like you are in so much pain. She called to order me something stronger. Once it was delivered, she helped me to my room to take a shower and to bed. I stayed in the mental hospital for about four days before I had to see the doctor. Once I saw the doctor, it was two other people in his office. A female and another male, the doctor asked me how I was feeling. I sat up in the wheelchair straight, and while looking into his eyes, I told him what had brought me to the ER initially.

I used every medical term that I had learned in anatomy class and EMT/paramedic school to show him that I had good sense and that I was not suicidal by no means, just in chronic pain. He listened to me with a look of amazement on his face. I had described my surgery and condition to the tee.

Once I was finished, the doctor stated, "I am so sorry, you are not supposed to be here in this facility. That my problem is chronic pain, not psych."

He stated that he was going to write a letter and put it into my medical records. Also, the female that was in the room stated that she was going to write a letter to the specialist that is going to perform the implant and the insurance company.

Next, the doctor asked me, "Did you have someone to come and pick you up?"

I stated, "Yes."

My oldest daughter picked me up and took me home. Once the third specialist contacted me with the surgery date, I had the device implanted into my body for chronic pain. The doctor had to turn the frequency so high just to reach the damage in my right foot. I was walking like a person who had just had a stroke.

The doctor asked me, "Did you know why you were referred to me?"

I stated, "No…"

He stated that the first two surgeons got into it concerning something that the first doctor had done. So the second surgeon referred me back to him, and he refused to touch me. I'm still drugged up trying to understand what was going on. I told the doctor that I was rushed by ambulance because of a near drug overdose. He said that he couldn't just take me off the medication abruptly. I could have withdrawal symptoms. I was still in chronic pain even after the implant. I was so drugged up; I had two near overdoses due to my specialist just adding to the medication that the previous doctor had prescribed me.

It took my family doctor to review my medications to tell me that several medications didn't go together and that he was taking me off them. Sadly, four years, three months, and a day since I had the back surgery. I was having outpatient surgery to have the neurostimulator removed from my body. This makes it the sixth back surgery that I had to endure. I really can't explain the amount of pain and suffering that my body and mind had to endure. All because my first surgeon decided, in my opinion, because of greed. He delayed my emergency surgery!

No human should have to go through what I have, period! I have been going through different emotions. Trying to figure out why me. I began to say, why not me; I only say that because through all my pain and suffering, I have kept my mind stayed on Jesus! Oh yes! I have tried to find a lawyer that would represent me, but no one would represent me. He was either on their board, they were working with him on a case, or it was a conflict of interest. One lawyer told me to go out of town. I am on disability with no money to pay a lawyer. At times, I felt discouraged. However, I refused to let him destroy my life!

James 5:15 KJV And the prayer of faith shall save the sick, and the Lord shall raise him up; and if he have committed sins, they shall be forgiven him.

Chapter 6

The First Year of Pain

I was referred to the fourth specialist. He viewed my records, and he determined that my body produces a lot of scar tissue. So he ordered a myelogram test. Sadly, it revealed that I had an extreme amount of scar tissue. So the plan that was discussed with me was scar tissue removal. However, the day before the surgery, the nurse told me that I was having re-ruptured disc surgery.

I said, "Oh no, the doctor said that he was removing scar tissue."

She said, "No, ma'am."

I became extremely depressed all over again. I went to see my dad, and I told him that I couldn't do this again. I couldn't go through the nerve pain, physical therapy, or depression. I told my youngest son, who was in the navy at the time, that I couldn't do this again. Meaning going through nonstop pain. I had the fourth surgery, and to my surprise, I didn't have the excruciating pain right after surgery. I literally had two weeks of pain-free healing. I was so happy. I told anyone that would listen to me. However, around the third week, the pain slowly came back.

My last appointment with this doctor ended with sad news. He told me that he couldn't do anything else for me. I immediately became upset; I asked the doctor frantically who was going to be my doctor. He stated that I couldn't have another surgery on my back. Unfortunately, he was not accurate with that statement. It would be a year and six months before my disc ruptured again. This makes the third time with a total of six surgeries on my back within five years. If the doctors that saw me as a patient were friends of the first doctor. It's sad that they wouldn't try and fix me. It was as if it was all about getting paid.

I have become disabled, depressed, and angry. How many times could a disc rupture? What did they remove out of my disc each time it ruptured? This is ridiculous for a person to suffer as I had! What did they do wrong? Did they even care about me as a patient? Did they go on vacation with the money that they made from my failed surgeries? Did they even care that I was suffering and in severe pain? It took a new young surgeon to help me. However, I'm left with gross limitations, chronic pain, and stiffness daily. I wished that I had met him first to perform my emergency surgery.

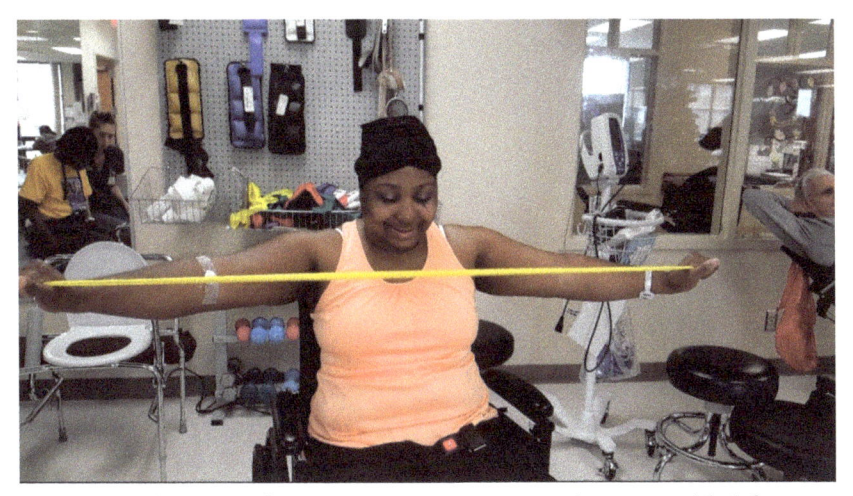

I was determined not to quit nor give up on living a viable life! God has things for me to do in this life. Lying in bed drugged up every day was not going to be me anymore PERIOD!

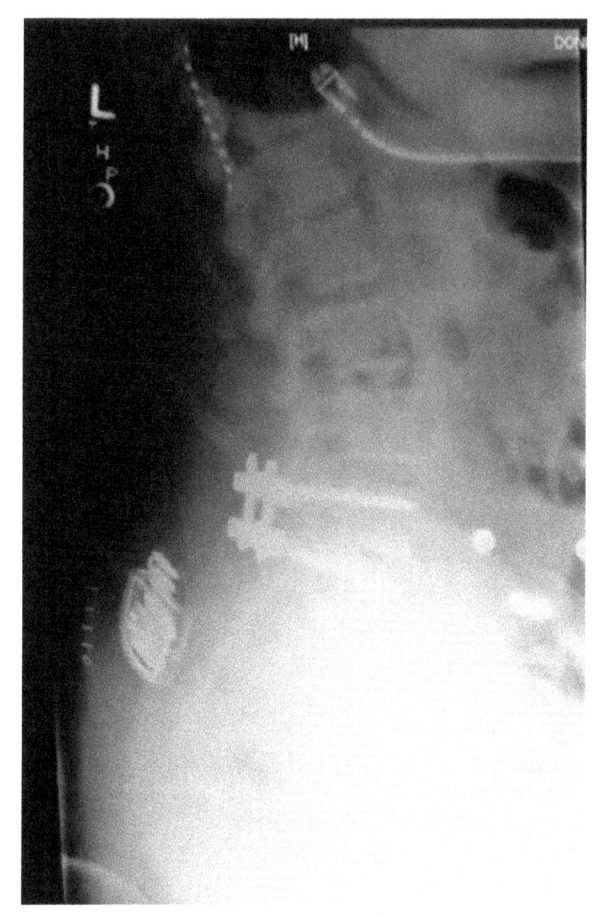

They say a picture speaks a thousand words. I chose to share my X-ray with the world. This picture shows where my physical pain started. Also, it represents my pain and healing all in one. The screws you see are literally holding my skeleton together. The square object was powering the device that was supposed to help my excruciating pain. However, it did not work. So, it has was removed shortly after my screws were implanted. Sadly, I still suffer with pain, not as severe. I have learned how to live with the pain. Some of the alternative measures I use to take the place of pain medication is aquatic therapy, line dancing and just staying active doing something daily. I make adjustments as needed of course.

Chapter 7

My Acceptance

I began to accept the chronic pain, my disability, and my limitations. I have realized that it was because of God that I made it through these horrifying five years of back surgeries. I started trying to act like I was normal. I tried to push myself to do things that I used to do. I began to keep my mind on the Lord, reading my Bible and encouraging others. One thing that really surprised me was how much I love sewing. It really took my mind off the pain. I enrolled in college as a PCT with my youngest daughter. I maintained a 4.0 average, and I was really enjoying getting out of the house. While trying to complete my clinical toward the end. I began to experience dull pain on the left side of my disc. I was able to complete my clinical hours.

Unfortunately, one Friday night, my daughter took me to the ER. I was in so much pain they gave me a cocktail of pain medications. I literally slept until Monday. When I had awakened, the pain had traveled down my left leg. I immediately knew what it was; I started crying, and I called my mama. I told her that I couldn't walk. I called the ambulance, and I was taken to the ER again. They gave me some more medication, not as much as before. The doctor referred me to one of the best neurosurgeons in my state. I was able to get an appointment within two days. At my appointment, my new doctor looked at my records and ordered another myelogram and x-ray. Once he reviewed the results, he determined that he had to perform surgery to fuse my two discs together.

I said, "Let's do it!"

He scheduled the surgery and performed the surgery. I was taking it very easy; I had screws and rods literally holding my spine together. I didn't know what I was about to experience. It would be something that was worse than the beginning.

With Jesus on my side nothing else mattered. He was with me when some people left or thought that I would be handicap and my life was washed up. Oh, but no Jesus was the reason for that smile.

Chapter 8

The Unforeseen Pain

After my fifth back surgery, September 20, 2016. I was hospitalized for four days, and I was discharged home. The first couple of weeks, I took it easy. But one night, I tried to move. I had the most excruciating pain that was far worse than the 270-plus days of pain that I had experienced a few years earlier. It was as if I was being electrocuted. Every night after the sun went down, I had to take my shower and get ready for bed. I was bracing myself for this horrifying pain. It was as if I had exchanged the severe sciatic nerve pain for a level of pain that I didn't know existed.

I called the surgeon's office several times, asking that someone tell me what to expect. I was having spasms that were waking me up out of my sleep, screaming. I let out a shout that I didn't know was within me. I would lie in bed and wait for my youngest daughter, Kenya, to come home. One night, I called her on the cell phone, asking her to please come help me.

She would say, "Ma, I'm seven minutes away."

I would have to go to the restroom so bad. I would hold it; I had steps by my bed. I would ease out of bed. I would cry and shake as if I was cold. But the pain was so great that I was so afraid of the pain.

She would say, "Hold on to me, Ma, I got you."

With her little petite body, she would guide me to the shower or toilet. I would scoot because I was in so much pain. I would cry, Lord, please help me! I was trying so hard to keep my modesty. It was so hard, but I didn't want my family to feel like they had to take care of me. The spasms keep coming every night for about a couple of months like clockwork! I stayed in my room, shutting myself away from the world. Simply because I knew that no one could help me. I didn't feel sorry for myself, nor did I blame God. I had to endure this pain for a reason. My strength was coming from the Lord, God of Israel!

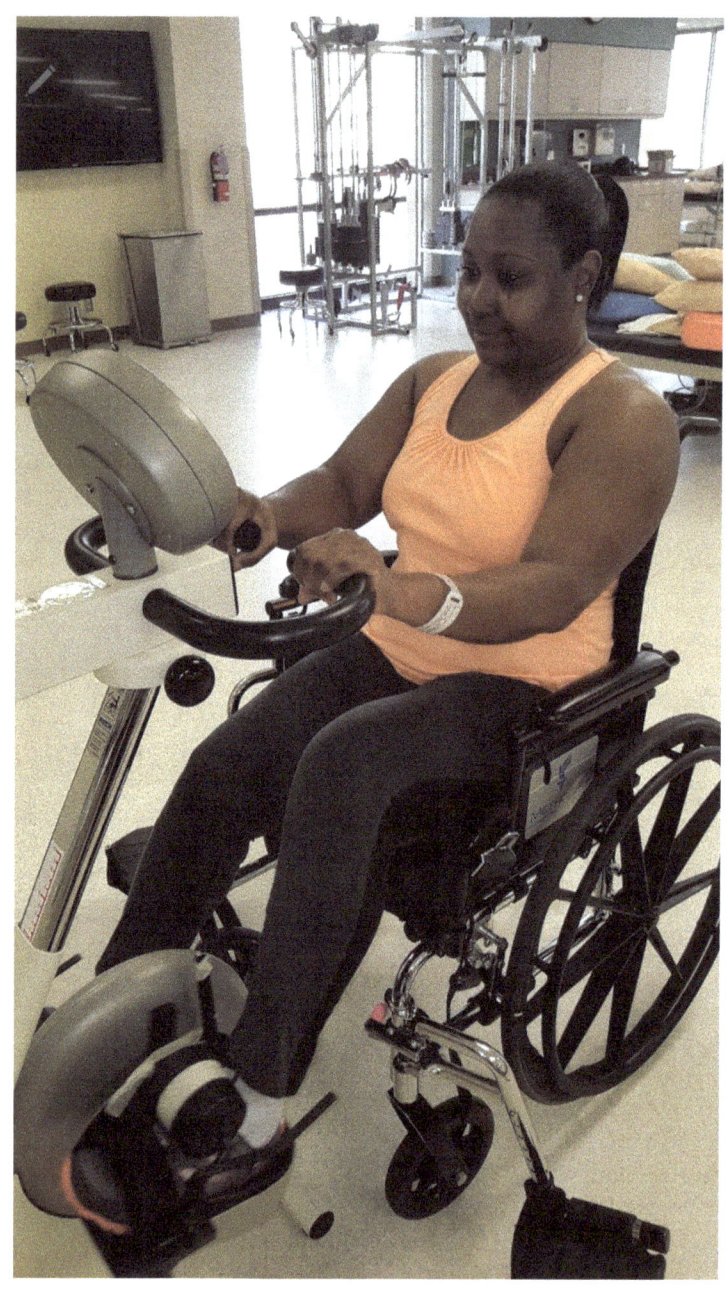

Stay focused and work hard in the end you will see good results. Only if you all could see me now!

1 Corinthians 13:7 KJV Beareth all things, believeth all things, hopeth all things, endureth all things.

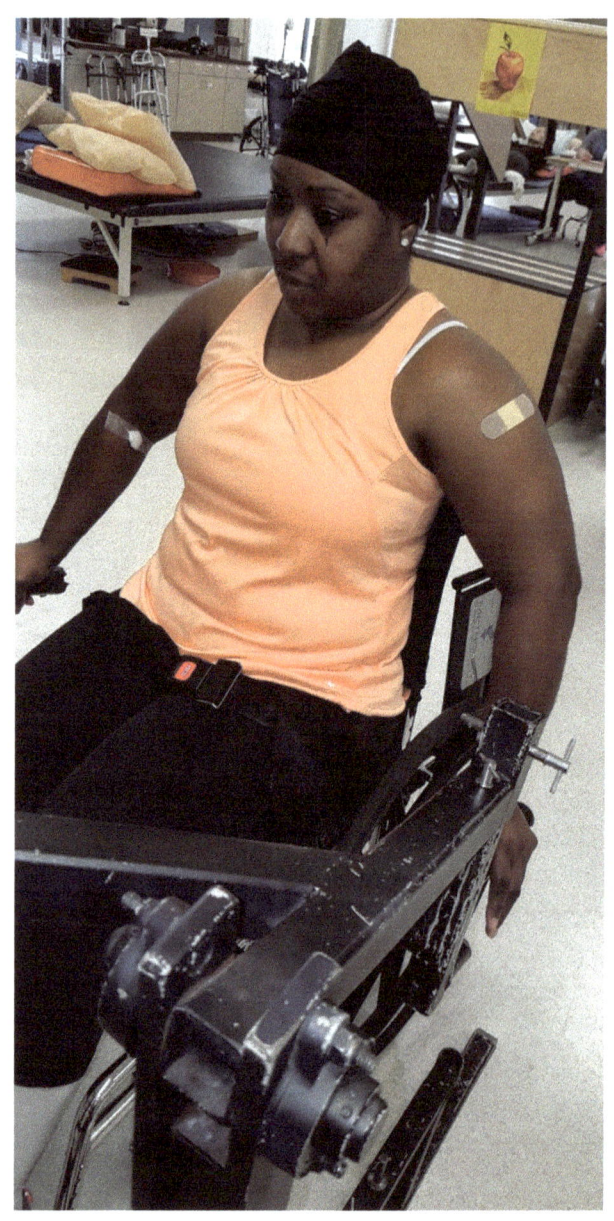

I was pushing through the medication and pain. Staying focused, thinking about getting better and my future. I didn't know what was ahead. I put all my faith in God. I had to put in the work.

CHAPTER 9
My Feeling of Abandonment

All while I was going through this pain and surgeries. I still wanted to be in a relationship. I still wanted to be in love. Sadly, it was as if every guy that seemed to be interested in me, they spoke highly of my character. Some have even said that I would make someone a good wife one day. Also that I was a good person. I guess not for them; as soon as a guy realized the extent of my surgeries and that I was disabled, they shied away from me, literally stopped calling or coming by.

The feeling of rejection hurts so bad. I began to notice the signs right away. I guess that they felt that they would have to take care of me. Sadly, that wasn't the case. I feel that a man that truly wanted to be with me wouldn't let my limitations or disability influence their decision to be in a relationship with me. To be alone during this life-changing experience sucks so bad. I cried many nights, wishing that I had someone to be by my side and to hold me when I was hurting. Someone to just say I'm here for you or I got you.

Even someone to go to the hospital ER, doctor's visits, or surgeries.

Unfortunately, I didn't have that type of support. I long for a mate that would love me despite of my disability. You can't judge a book by its cover. I don't look disabled, and a person wouldn't know unless I told them. I hurt every day. When someone asks me how I am feeling. I always say I'm working it out. Just to keep from lying or sounding so depressed.

Sometimes I feel like I'm going to be alone for the rest of my life. All because a doctor decided to wait over nineteen hours to perform an emergency back surgery on me five years ago. It has caused me so much grief and pain. I wonder what if he had performed my surgery when it was scheduled, would my situation be better? Would I be remarried? Would I be traveling the country as I did before the surgery? I don't know.

Chapter 10

My Faith

I thank God for everything and his breath of life. I know that I sounded like I was all in my feelings. Please don't misconstrue how I was feeling. I do have faith that God would bring me through this challenging time in my life. It was his word and my church family that helped to keep me encouraged and positive concerning my illness.

It was the phone calls, texts, Facebook, visits, prayers, and Scriptures that helped me get through this difficult time in my life. Truth be told, I really do know why I'm going through so much pain. I believe that I am an Israelite. The Israelite of the Bible. Simply because I read Deuteronomy, twenty-eighth chapter. It talks about the blessing and the curses of a nation of people.

Well, we are not experiencing the blessing that is written in Deuteronomy 28:1–14. However, we are surely experiencing the curses written in Deuteronomy 28:15–68. I truly believe that my experience is spiritual. I am suffering for a reason. Don't get me wrong; I have been blessed to gain knowledge of God's word. My church family nationwide has helped me financially. This was truly a blessing while sick, bedridden, or while I was in and out of the hospital. Not being able to work or pay my bills.

I am grateful indeed. Imagine not caring about anything but the pain, stopping. I used to talk to the pain as it was a person. Telling it to stop, leave me alone! I would cry out to God, and I asked him to help me. After the first surgery, I asked him to help me. I'm still in my right mind; I'm fighting each day to get stronger. I know that it was my faith that kept me from losing my mind and giving up. Oh, giving up was not an option. Because I know that the Lord has work for me to do. Also, my children, grandchildren, and family need me.

I have been told that I am a strong woman. I will not take credit because I know that my strength comes from the Lord. I am nothing without him. I give him all the praise and the glory for my life and the pain. I realize that I rather have my pain and suffering now than later. I believe that everything happens for a reason.

Only God could have brought me through the hell that I have been through the last five years of pain. Let me expound on the word *hell*; I am using it in this text. It's hell to hurt twenty-four-seven nonstop. It was hell when I was lying in bed alone in severe pain day and night. It's hell when I was so drugged up and didn't know that I was in this world. It's hell that I wasn't working and bills had to be paid. It's hell when I don't remember anything in 2013 because I was so lethargic. It's hell when nobody around me understand the pain that I was trying to endure. The word *hell* is a state of condition. I was truly going through hell!

Oh, the Lord had me. My mama took me to an organization that paid my light bill for a year. My church paid my rent in full a couple of times. They brought me food; oh, how this has humbled me. Because all my life, I was a giver. Now, I had to accept help in any form however it came to me. At this point in my life, people that knew me before my surgery knew that I worked for whatever I wanted. I was a hairstylist for twenty-seven years, an EMT for five years, and a paramedic graduate. Also, I owned nine salons within nineteen years of doing hair. I worked for the state for five years and the federal government for two years.

At forty-four years old, my life changed drastically forever. I have been fighting daily to just keep my independence and modesty. As long as God gives me his breath of life every morning. It hurts me to see my youngest daughter work so hard to try and help me. She is working a job and trying to stay focused on getting into nursing school. I can't help her with a dime to pay for school. I have faith that God will make a way for us both.

Chapter 11

A Lifetime of Pain

This is a lifestyle change for me. I don't know what my future holds for me. I know that this experience has brought me closer to God. I'm trying daily to be obedient to his word. I'm actually living moment by moment. I can't worry about anything that I can't change. I hurt every day, and I am trying to stay focused on what my purpose in life is and to share my story. Also, to tell the world how good God is to those who believe and obey his every word.

Pain is a part of my life, but I will no longer let it take over my life. God gave me his breath of life, and only he can and will take it from me when he is ready. Pain is pain, I would say. If I don't endure it, who's going to? I must stay focused on the breath that God gives me every day. I can't make it if I don't.

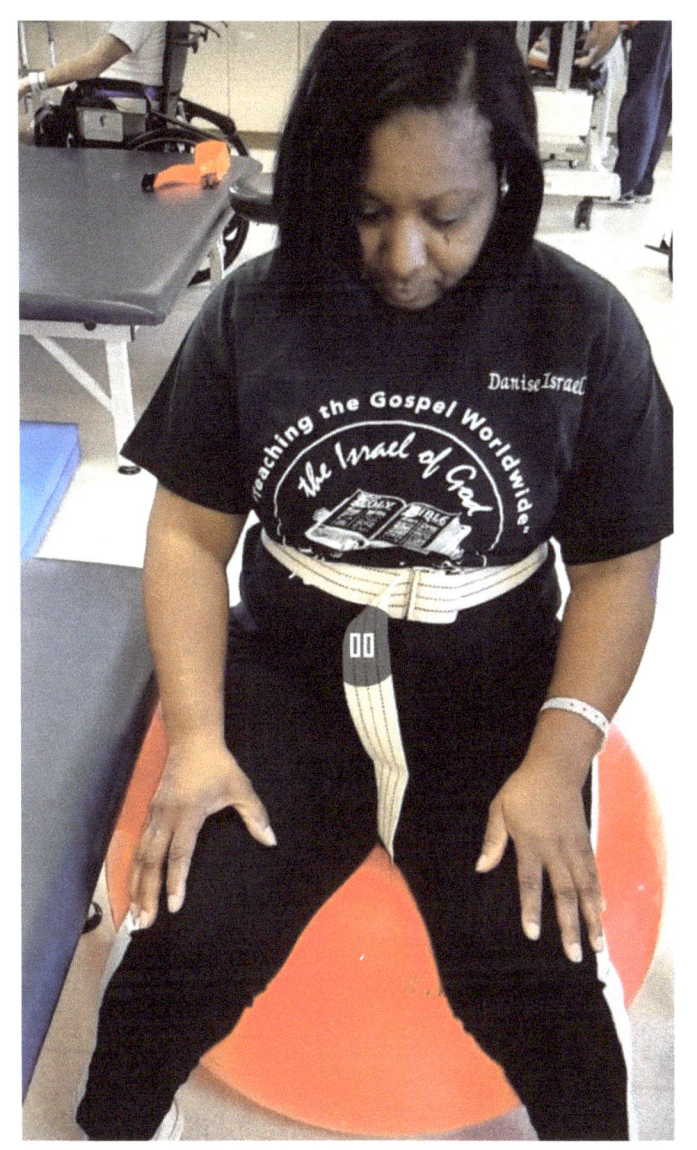

I couldn't let the pain control me. I had to get my strength back and walk again. I had to be able to do basic things for myself. I just took one day at a time. If I didn't do it, it wasn't going to be done. God gave me this gift of life. I had to take care of his temple. I was on a mission. Failing was not an option.

At the end of the day, it's all about Jesus. Not what people might think. Money, material things, or this world. I tell you while I was on my sickbed, wanting the pain to stop. Those things don't mean nothing to me. I was trying to just endure the pain. I knew that death was not an option, period! I have learned to deal with the pain. Pain will no longer take over my mind and body. I will not complain because there are others truly worse off than me. In my pain, I thought about others. That helped me push through it even until this day.

Chapter 12
Oh, My Israelite Sistas

Oh, I didn't go through this pain alone. I had a great support system. A group of awesome women in my life. I will be mentioning a few that was there for me through my darkest, unbearable times. Many nights in my first year of this horrific surgery, Sister Tiara from Terry, Mississippi, she's like my little sister. I would call her all times of the day and night crying.

I would be hurting so bad she would say, "I sure hate that you are going through so much pain."

She would come and sit with me after Sabbath class. When I couldn't attend. She would always lend an ear even if she couldn't understand what I was saying. In 2015, I met Sister Margaret in Melbourne, Florida. She is like a blood sister to me. She was there for me to lend her ear and encourage spiritual words. She had cried with me many nights. Her voice is so calming and angelic to me, if I may say. She is one of the kindest and loving person that I know. So many times, I would call her to vent, cry, or scream. Because I was in so much pain.

Around the first week in December 2016. A sister called me because she had gotten my number from Sister Drew in Chicago. Sister Drew had posted on Facebook to keep my Israelite Church family all over the country informed of my condition. However, she never posted what my medical condition was specifically. So Sister Cheryl in Dallas, Texas, called me the moment I felt I was about to have a nervous breakdown. Literally, I didn't know who to call; I couldn't reach anyone that I tried to call. When I heard her voice, and she asked me what my illness was, I told her about the multiple back surgeries. We could relate to each other immediately. She has had the same back surgeries. Our first back surgeries were done in the same month and year. Wow, finally, someone could really understand my pain! I thank Jesus!

The last time I really broke down was December 13, 2016. I had awakened around 5:00 a.m. I was hungry. I decided to cook some cheese grits. I had been nauseated for about a week. I was so weak. I turned on the stove. I could hardly stand. I went to my bathroom, and I set on my walker. I looked at myself in the mirror. I admitted that I needed help! I began to cry. I called my daughter Kenya on her cell phone to come help me! I told her to call Mama or somebody because I couldn't do this anymore. She called Mama, and I remembered crying hysterically. I called to hear sister Margaret's voice. It was around 6 a.m. central time zone and 7:00 a.m. eastern time zone her time. I called her deeply depressed, and I felt like my life was leaving my body. I kept telling her that I couldn't do it anymore. I need help! She couldn't do nothing but start praying for me. I gave the phone to my daughter Kenya.

I was so weak, and my legs were going out on me. I eased down onto the floor. Because I couldn't move to the right or left. I rolled from side to side, crying out to the Lord to please help me!

I screamed so loud my mama said, "Baby, just take the medicine."

I told her that it was not working! I told my daughter to call my sister Shonda in Texas. She and my daughter started praying over the phone. I looked at the clock, and it was almost 8:00 a.m. While lying on Kenya's lap, I told her that I couldn't do this anymore. I told her that I wasn't giving up. I just needed help. Because I couldn't take the pain or take care of myself anymore.

I told her to call the surgeon's office at 8:00 a.m. She had gotten the nurse on the line. I told her that I was hurting so bad and that I was crying out for help. She told me to call the pain specialist. Also, if I was hurting so badly, to go to the ER. We had to look up the number for the pain specialist. I was talking to the nurse, and she told me that they couldn't do anything until they received my medical records. It has already been over one month, and they haven't received them. She told me to call and try and expedite sending them my records. Really, I told my mama that I was going to take a shower. Afterward, call the ambulance. Once the ambulance had arrived, it was one of my old coworkers. He took good care of me until we made it to the ER. The hospital was on diversion.

He said, "Danise, I don't care, they are going to see you."

Once we had entered the ER, I had to wait in the hallway for a few minutes. He found a room that had reclining chairs. He and his partner helped put me in the chair. I was hurting so bad and severely depressed. I couldn't stop crying. I called Sister Akemi; I was so glad that I called her. She has this calming and caring voice too. She asked me what can I do for you? I said I don't know. She asked me if I thought that rehabilitation would help me. Immediately a light bulb went off in my head. I said yes! That's exactly what I needed. I felt so much better. I had the solution to my situation. It was time for me to have physical and occupational therapy.

The nurse and ER doctor came to see me immediately. I told the doctor that I was depressed. I was in chronic pain, not psych.

He said, "I understand."

Also, I told him that they could send me across the street to the mental hospital or admit me into the medical hospital. Going home was not an option.

He said, "Let me go call your surgeon."

A nurse came back to give me some pain medication.

Another person came in and said, "Oh, you are being admitted into the main hospital."

I said, "Okay…," for about four days, I was kept in an observation room.

I guess until they had decided what to do with or for me. I felt calm and relieved that everyone was on the same page as I was. The staff took good care of me. My surgeon and his nurse practitioner came every day to see me. He said that it was just time for some intense physical therapy. My blood pressure is now 119/80. When I was in the ER, my pressure was 198/90. I was truly at peace.

The social worker gave me a list of nursing homes to choose from. I looked at them very carefully. I knew where each one was. I looked them all up, and they had a three-star rating.

I immediately said, "Nope, a nursing home is not an option for me."

I needed to get into the Methodist Rehabilitation Hospital, period. Oh, how negative the social worker and another administrator were toward me getting into that facility.

I said, "Ma'am, I have faith that I would get in."

I was told on several occasions that they didn't accept my insurance. I immediately called the insurance company. I asked the agent to call to see if they accepted my insurance.

She immediately came back and said, "Yes, ma'am, they do, and they have a bed."

I pressed the call button and asked my nurse to send the social worker back into my room. Once she came into my room, I told her with confidence that I was going to get into the rehabilitation hospital. Also, they accepted my insurance, and they had a bed available. *Huh…* I'm a child of the most high God! He has my back! Next, they sent a psychiatrist to my room. Okay, here we go again. Well… I did tell them that I was depressed. I get it. He asked me if any of my medications had been increased.

I said, "Uh…no! Okay, you increase my medication, my mind is altered, and I fall in the middle of the night, and my daughter finds me on the floor. Uh… No! That doesn't make sense. My condition is not psych, it's musculoskeletal."

He said, "Well, there is nothing I could do for you."

I said, "Yes, I know."

He politely got up off the couch and headed toward the door.

He looked back at me, and I said, "Long as God gives me his breath of life each morning, I will be just fine."

He said, "That's a very nice attitude to have."

The next day or so, the social worker came by my room again.

She said, "Ms. Donerson, can you please pick one of the nursing homes listed just in case you don't get into the rehabilitation hospital?"

Once again, I said, "No, I have faith that I am going to get in."

She said, "I don't want you to be mad if you don't."

I looked at her with a smile; she said, "Okay." And walked out of my room.

I wasn't playing with these people! A lady called my cell phone. For some reason, she said that she couldn't find my hospital room. She called both of my daughters before she got me on the phone. She asked me a lot of questions concerning my situation.

She said, "Well, you qualify to get into the rehabilitation hospital."

However, she was waiting for the nurse with the insurance company to approve me.

She said, "Oh... Don't worry because I deal with your insurance company every day. I have your paperwork that the hospital had faxed over to me."

It would be Monday before she heard back from anyone. Monday came no answer. Oh, but Tuesday, the social worker came to my room with a look of amazement on her face.

"Well... Ms. Donerson, you got in!"

I started to say you didn't know! Sarcastically, but I didn't. I just smiled because I knew that God allowed me to get in concerning the odds that were against me. I was evaluated for rehab and approved. Now it was time for my transfer; I was so ready!

Chapter 13

My Intense Therapy

This was a new day for me, the day I entered the rehabilitation hospital. I was greeted by old coworkers and supervisors. I felt like a celebrity, oh yes! My room was like a suite, big and spacious. Once I was assessed and settled. I called my mama and told her not to worry about coming to visit me at the facility because I was in town, and I was going to receive the intense physical therapy that I needed. I had an awesome steak dinner; I felt so great I finally was about to get the help that I had to scream and shout to get. Well, after a good night sleep. Oh, it was on. Let the therapy begin. No, seriously! They worked every inch of my body from head to toe, literally! That was okay; I told the staff that I was there to work not play.

I had therapy every day for three hours. The nurse had to get me up out of bed. They gave me my pain medication and muscle relaxer before each session. Boy, did I need it! I was okay with it. I was doing this for myself so that I could gain my independence back. I had to learn how to bathe myself, put my clothes and shoes on, walk, stand, go upstairs, and get into a car again. I worked very hard, and

I thank the team of physical and occupational therapists for doing an awesome job. I thank God for allowing me to be at one of the top rehabilitation hospitals in the country. They truly had some state-of-the-art equipment.

I was in the hospital for about a month. I had never been admitted into a hospital that long. Everyone was so amazed at the progress that I was making. Some couldn't believe the drive that I had. People don't understand that I owe God my life. This life, his life! I have been through hell dealing with this pain and surgeries. God truly knows how much that we can bear. God knows that I couldn't do this by myself.

I remember seeing a woman sitting in her wheelchair. Both of us were waiting for the therapist. We were both side by side in our wheelchair. Oh yes, I was bound to a wheelchair. However, I knew that it was going to be temporary. Now I would see how sad she looked each day. I couldn't stand it anymore. I had to say something to her. I finally got my chance.

I said to her, "Ma'am, can I talk to you?"

She looked up at me and said, "Yes."

I leaned in my chair and held her hand, and I said, "How old are you?"

She said, "Forty-five."

I said, "I'm forty-eight."

I asked her, "Did she have any kids?"

She said, "Yes. They are grown."

I said, "Me too."

Her left leg was amputated from the knee down. I told her both of our kids are grown. Let's do this for ourselves.

When everybody around us is gone, we need to be able to take care of ourselves.

She smiled; I said, "Every day, come in this gym and do your best, even if it was a one-pound weight. Just do something from that day on."

I felt her staring at me doing my therapy. She was doing hers too every day. One day I saw her standing on one leg, walking with her walker. I felt so much joy inside for her. I knew that she was going to be okay. I met some wonderful friends. I have never been a quitter, and I sure couldn't give up now!

CHAPTER 14

Pain You Are Evicted!

I was discharged home on January 4, 2017. Kenya picked me up from the hospital. I was so happy to see my baby girl! She has had my back literally. Once I was home, I felt so great. I started doing things around the house. Unpacking my bags, washing my clothes. I have regained my independence back. I have been taking every day, one moment at a time. I still hurt every day. I have learned to push through the pain. If a person has not been through this type of pain before, they won't understand.

This has been a long journey for me and my family, who were here for me. I have regained my confidence, motivation, strength, sanity, and hope back. I have faith that God will continue to bring me through any situation that I may encounter as long as I stay obedient to his word. I can't do nothing in and of myself. I have learned to totally depend on Jesus, period. This experience has humbled me tremendously. If a person thinks that they can endure pain of any kind without God, they are mistaken.

DANISE DONERSON

I'm standing tall, God has healed my mind and body. You are looking at a walking testimony. No matter what type of pain you are going through. Decide in your mind what you are going to do. It is totally up to you. I decided that I wanted to live and I cried out to God and he heard me. Today I live for him. I'm taking care of myself daily, by getting up moving around doing something. I refuse to lie down daily doing nothing. It helps my body from getting stiff and hurting so bad. Yes, I still hurt. However, I have learned to live with the state my body is in now. I do things to keep it from getting worse. Take charge of your life. Take care of you! Stop letting the cares of this world bring you down. During my sickness a lot of people that were in my life left. Truth be told they were never in my life. They were fair weather friends. Oh, put I have a friend that sticketh closer than a brother, Jesus. He is all that I really need. Whoever you are be proactive about your health. Start eating right talk to your doctor about an alternative to pain medications. Try aquatic therapy, research and find out some things that works for you that relieves your pain. I knew that I couldn't function being drugged up all day every day. So, I stopped taking pain pills. All I can say is that's when I start living. Now I'm living a viable life and functioning much better. My journey took 10 years to be manageable without pain medication and constant physical therapy. Through it all God is still keeping me. I'm just enduring until the end.

I give my life to God because if it wasn't for him, I couldn't have made it. I can't say this enough. I must tell the world and leave proof of my struggle with the severe pain that I have endured for many to read about. Long after I'm gone from this world, I have written the story of my pain for people to know that there is hope, even if they may feel that they are alone.

At night, I hurt so bad when the severe spasms would hit me. While others slept in their beds silently. I screamed and cried out to God many nights. I slept with my Bible in my arms many days and nights. Pain can take over your mind if you let it. It almost took over mine. I believe that if I didn't have God's Word within me, I know that I couldn't have made it. I might not be alive today. Don't misconstrue what I'm saying; I never wanted to die.

The pain that I have endured, this is the best way that I can describe it. The pain was worse than I have depicted in this book. On a spiritual note, I feel that if I hadn't gone through this unforeseen pain, I would be lost in this world. This experience kept me focused on God and his Word. Even though I feel that my first surgeon was the cause of my severe pain. Simply because he waited nineteen hours to perform my emergency surgery. I just might have not gone through this crippling pain.

I pray to God that I never have to experience this pain ever again in my life. Just sitting back and trying to recall every moment bring tears to my eyes. Chills cover my body from head to toe. However, I never asked God why me; I was never angry with God for allowing me to suffer as I did; instead, I thank him for the pain. Because it just might have saved my life.

I have cried out to God to take this excruciating pain from me. So he put it in my mind to write in this book all of my pain and tears from every single night. My account is written down. It is therapy for me. Until this day, I cannot remember the pain. God took it from my body and mind. The words written on these pages cannot do it justice. I have done my best to depict my suffering. This was my Job experience, and God was truly in control. He was the only one that could have performed this miracle. No matter what type of pain you may be going through in your life, you can and will get through it. Remember, Job's health, family, and finances were restored. Endure it until the end. You can and will do it. Do it for yourself. You are worth it. You are special and wonderfully made in God's image with a purpose.

Pain, you are evicted! You are evicted from my life, my body, and my mind! Leave and don't come back again! You will not control me anymore! The Lord, God of Israel, has my back now; I pray that my story helps somebody endure their pain, whatever it may be.

Just keep trusting God and cry out to Him.

About the Author

At the time this book was written, I was forty-eight years old. Also, I'm the mother of four beautiful children: Lakendra (William), Jerome, Delance (Tara), and Kenya (Timothy). My thirteen grandchildren: Major, Kendarian, Malcolm, Kourianna, De'Sean, Victoria, Jaden, Jordan, Jamari'a, Jamari, Lil Jerome, Jayylon, and Bleu (Major).

I am a retired hairstylist for thirty-three years and EMT for five years and a paramedic graduate. I'm from Jackson, Mississippi. This is the second book that I have written to encourage others to endure until the end, to never give in to their pain.